The ESSENTIALS® of
REGISTERED TRADEMARK

LINEAR ALGEBRA

**Staff of Research and Education Association,
Dr. M. Fogiel, Director**

GW00374853

Research and Education Association
61 Ethel Road West
Piscataway, New Jersey 08854

THE ESSENTIALS OF LINEAR ALGEBRA®

Printed in the United States of America

Library of Congress Catalog Card Number 87-61804

International Standard Book Number 0-87891-610-5

Revised Printing, 1990

ESSENTIALS is a registered trademark of
Research and Education Association, Piscataway, New Jersey 08854

WHAT "THE ESSENTIALS" WILL DO FOR YOU

This book is a review and study guide. It is comprehensive and it is concise.

It helps in preparing for exams, in doing homework, and remains a handy reference source at all times.

It condenses the vast amount of detail characteristic of the subject matter and summarizes the **essentials** of the field.

It will thus save hours of study and preparation time.

The book provides quick access to the important facts, principles, theorems, concepts, and equations of the field.

Materials needed for exams, can be reviewed in summary form — eliminating the need to read and re-read many pages of textbook and class notes. The summaries will even tend to bring detail to mind that had been previously read or noted.

This "ESSENTIALS" book has been carefully prepared by educators and professionals and was subsequently reviewed by another group of editors to assure accuracy and maximum usefulness.

Dr. Max Fogiel
Program Director

CONTENTS

CHAPTER 1

LINEAR MATRICES

I.I LINEAR EQUATIONS AND MATRICES

A linear equation is an equation of the form $A_1X_1+A_2X_2+\ldots+A_NX_N = b$, where $A_1,\ldots,A_N$ and b are real constants.

Examples: a) $2x+6y=9$ b) $x_1+3x_2+7x_3=5$ c) $\alpha-2=0$

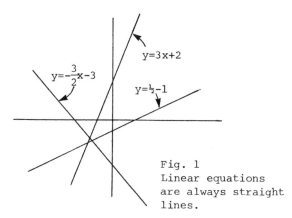

$y=3x+2$

$y=-\frac{3}{2}x-3$

$y=\frac{1}{2}-1$

Fig. 1
Linear equations
are always straight
lines.

A system of linear equations is a finite set of linear equations, all of which use the same set of variables.

1

Examples: a) $2x_1 + x_2 + 5x_3 = 4$ b) $y - z = 5$

$$x_2 + 3x_3 = 0 \qquad z = 1$$

$$7x_1 + 3x_2 + x_3 = 9$$

The solution of a system of linear equations is that set of real numbers which, when substituted into the set of variables, satisfies each equation in the system. The set of all solutions is called the solution set S of the system.

Examples: a) $x_1 + x_2 = 5$ S= $\{(5,0),(0,5),(4,1),(1,4)(3,2),$
(2,3)$\}$

b) $y + z = 9$ S= $\{5,4\}$

$$z = 4$$

A consistent system of linear equations has at least one solution, while an inconsistent system has no solutions.

Examples: a) $y + z = 9$ S= $\{5,4\}$ (consistent system)
$z = 4$

b) $x_1 + x_2 = 7$ S= ϕ (inconsistent system)
$x_1 = 3$
$x_1 - x_2 = 7$

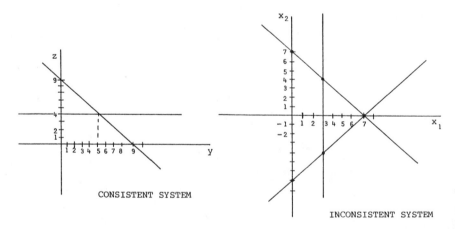

CONSISTENT SYSTEM

INCONSISTENT SYSTEM

Every system of linear equations has either one solution, no solution, or infinitely many solutions.

The augmented matrix for a system of linear equations is the matrix of the form:

$$\begin{bmatrix} a_{11} & a_{12} & \dots & a_{1N} & b_1 \\ a_{21} & a_{22} & \dots & a_{2N} & b_2 \\ \vdots & & & & \\ a_{M1} & a_{M2} & \dots & a_{MN} & b_M \end{bmatrix}$$

where a_{ij} represents each coefficient in the system and b_i represents each constant in the system.

Example:

$$\begin{aligned} x_1 + 6x_2 - 2x_3 &= 4 \\ 3x_1 \quad + \quad x_3 &= 7 \\ 5x_1 - 3x_2 + x_3 &= 0 \end{aligned} \qquad \begin{bmatrix} 1 & 6 & -2 & 4 \\ 3 & 0 & 1 & 7 \\ 5 & -3 & 1 & 0 \end{bmatrix}$$

Elementary row operations are operations on the rows of an augmented matrix, which are used to reduce that matrix to a more solvable form. These operations are the following:

a) Multiply a row by a non-zero constant.

b) Interchange two rows.

c) Add a multiple of one row to another row.

1.2 HOMOGENEOUS SYSTEMS OF LINEAR EQUATIONS

A homogeneous system of linear equations is a system in which all of the constant terms (those which are not multiplied by any variables) are zero.

Example: $x_1 + 3x_2 = 0$ is a homogeneous system.

$$4x_1 + x_2 + 7x_3 = 0$$
$$2x_2 + 2x_3 = 0$$

Every homogeneous system of N linear equations has at last one solution, called the trivial solution, in which all of the variables $X_1, X_2, \dots, X_N$ are equal to zero. All other solutions to the system are called non-trivial solutions.

3

Every homogeneous system of linear equations has either (a) only the trivial solution, or (b) the trivial solution and an infinite number of non-trivial solutions. If there are more unknowns than equations, then the system has non-trivial solutions.

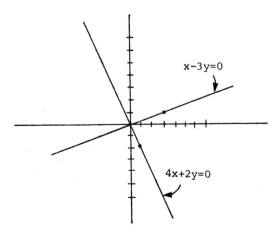

In a homogeneous system, all lines pass through origin.

1.3 MATRICES

A matrix is a rectangular array of numbers, called entries.

Examples: a) $\begin{bmatrix} 6 & 2 \\ 3 & 1 \\ 0 & 0 \end{bmatrix}$ b) $\begin{bmatrix} 3 \\ 1 \end{bmatrix}$ c) $[1\ 7\ 2\ 1]$

A matrix with N rows and N columns is called a square matrix of order N.

Example: $\begin{bmatrix} 2 & 10 & 1 \\ 6 & 2 & 9 \\ 3 & 3 & 7 \end{bmatrix}$ is a square matrix of order 3.

4

Two matrices are equal if they have the same size and the same entries.

Entries starting at the top left and proceeding to the bottom right of a square matrix are said to be on the main diagonal of that matrix.

Example: 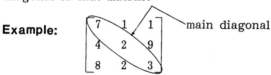 main diagonal

The sum B+D is the matrix obtained when two matrices, B and D, are added together; they must both be of the same size. B-D is obtained by subtracting the entries of D from the corresponding entries of B.

Examples: a) $\begin{bmatrix} 1 & 2 \\ 2 & 6 \end{bmatrix} + \begin{bmatrix} -4 & 7 \\ 1 & 1 \end{bmatrix} = \begin{bmatrix} -3 & 9 \\ 3 & 7 \end{bmatrix}$

$\qquad \qquad \quad$ B $\qquad \quad$ D

b) $\begin{bmatrix} 1 & 2 \\ 2 & 6 \end{bmatrix} - \begin{bmatrix} -4 & 7 \\ 1 & 1 \end{bmatrix} = \begin{bmatrix} 5 & -5 \\ 1 & 5 \end{bmatrix}$

The product of a matrix A by a scalar k is obtained by multiplying each entry of A by k.

Example: If $A = \begin{bmatrix} 4 & 7 \\ -1 & 2 \end{bmatrix}$ and k=3, then $Ak = \begin{bmatrix} 12 & 21 \\ -3 & 6 \end{bmatrix}$.

When multiplying two matrices A and B, the matrices (the number of columns of A must equal the number of rows of B) must be of the sizes M×N and N×P; to obtain the (ij) entry of AB, multiply the entries in row i of A by the corresponding entries in column j of B. Add up the resulting products; this sum is the (ij) entry of AB. If AB = C, then $C_{ij} = \sum\limits_{k=1}^{M} a_{ik} b_{kj}$.

Example:

If $A = \begin{bmatrix} 2 & 3 \\ 4 & 5 \end{bmatrix}$ and $B = \begin{bmatrix} 3 & 3 \\ 7 & 2 \end{bmatrix}$, then

$AB = \begin{bmatrix} 27 & 12 \\ 47 & 22 \end{bmatrix}$.

A matrix which contains entries corresponding to the coefficients of a system of linear equations, but excludes the constants of that system is called a coefficient matrix.

Example:

$$x_1 + 6x_2 - 2x_3 = 4$$
$$3x_1 + x_3 = 7$$
$$5x_1 - 3x_2 + x_3 = 0$$

$$\begin{bmatrix} 1 & 6 & -2 \\ 3 & 0 & 1 \\ 5 & -3 & 1 \end{bmatrix}$$

1.4 MATRIX ARITHMETIC

1.4.1 RULES OF MATRIX ARITHMETIC:

a) $A + B = B + A$ (Commutative Law of Addition)

b) $A + (B+C) = (A+B)+C$ (Associative Law of Addition)

c) $A(BC) = (AB)C$ (Associative Law of Multiplication)

d) $A(B\pm C) = AB \pm AC$ (Distributive Law)

e) $a(B+C) = aB + aC$

f) $(a\pm b)C = aC \pm bC$

g) $(ab)C = a(bC)$

h) $a(BC) = (aB)C = B(aC)$

A matrix whose entries are all zero is called a zero matrix, 0.

Examples:
a) $\begin{bmatrix} 0 & 0 \\ 0 & 0 \end{bmatrix}$
b) $\begin{bmatrix} 0 \\ 0 \\ 0 \end{bmatrix}$
c) $\begin{bmatrix} 0 & 0 & 0 \\ 0 & 0 & 0 \\ 0 & 0 & 0 \end{bmatrix}$

Theorem:

If the size of the matrices are such that the indicated operations can be performed, the following rules of matrix arithmetic are valid:

a) $A + 0 = 0 + A = A$

b) $A - A = 0$

c) $0 - A = -A$

d) $A0 = 0$

An identity matrix (I) is a square matrix with ones on the main diagonal and zeros everywhere else.

Examples: a) $\begin{bmatrix} 1 & 0 \\ 0 & 1 \end{bmatrix}$ b) $\begin{bmatrix} 1 & 0 & 0 & 0 \\ 0 & 1 & 0 & 0 \\ 0 & 0 & 1 & 0 \\ 0 & 0 & 0 & 1 \end{bmatrix}$

If A is a square matrix and a matrix B exists such that AB = BA = I, then A is invertible and B is the inverse of A, (A^{-1}). An invertible matrix has one and only one inverse.

Theorem:

If A and B are invertible matrices of the same size, then:

a) AB is invertible

b) $(AB)^{-1} = (A^{-1})(B^{-1})$

Formula for inverting a 2 × 2 matrix:

If A = $\begin{bmatrix} a & b \\ c & d \end{bmatrix}$, then $A^{-1} = \dfrac{1}{ad-bc} \begin{bmatrix} d & -b \\ -c & a \end{bmatrix}$.

Example:

If A = $\begin{bmatrix} 1 & 2 \\ 3 & 4 \end{bmatrix}$, then $A^{-1} = \begin{bmatrix} -2 & 1 \\ 1\frac{1}{2} & -\frac{1}{2} \end{bmatrix}$.

Theorem:

If A is an invertible matrix, then:

a) A^{-1} is invertible; $(A^{-1})^{-1} = A$

b) kA is invertible (where k is a non-zero scalar);
   $(kA)^{-1} = \dfrac{1}{k} A^{-1}$

c) A^N is invertible; $(A^N)^{-1} = (A^{-1})^N$

If A is a square matrix and x and y are integers, then:

a) $A^x A^y = A^{x+y}$

b) $(A^x)^y = A^{xy}$

1.5 GAUSSIAN ELIMINATION

A matrix is in reduced row-echelon form, if it has the following properties:

a) Either the first non-zero entry in a row is 1, or the row consists entirely of zeros.

b) All rows consisting entirely of zeros are grouped together at the bottom of the matrix.

c) If two successive rows do not consist entirely of zeros, then the leading 1 in the lower row occurs farther to the right than the leading 1 in the higher row.

d) Every column with a leading one has zeros in every other entry.

If a matrix has properties a, b and c, it is in row-echelon form.

Examples: a) The matrix $\begin{bmatrix} 1 & 0 & 0 & 4 \\ 0 & 1 & 1 & 2 \\ 0 & 0 & 0 & 1 \end{bmatrix}$ is in reduced row-echelon form.

b) The matrix $\begin{bmatrix} 1 & 4 & 0 & 3 \\ 0 & 1 & 0 & 0 \\ 0 & 0 & 1 & 2 \end{bmatrix}$ is in row-echelon form.

The variables corresponding to the leading ones in a reduced row-echelon matrix are called leading variables. Gauss-Jordan elimination is a process using elementary row operations by which any matrix can be brought into reduced row-echelon form. Once this is done the system of linear equations corresponding to that matrix is easily solvable. The process is as follows:

a) Find the leftmost column of the matrix not consisting entirely of zeros.

b) If necessary, switch the top row with another row so that a non-zero entry appears at the top of the column found in (a).

c) If necessary, multiply the top row by the inverse of the entry in that row which is also the top of the column found in (a). This is done so that this column has a leading one.

8

d) Add appropriate multiples of the first row to the rows below so that all entries below the leading one of the column found in (a) become zeros.

e) Cover the first row and, using the remaining submatrix, begin again at step (a). Continue (a) through (e) until the matrix is in row-echelon form.

f) Starting with the last row which does not consist entirely of zeros, add appropriate multiples of each row to the rows above so that each column containing a one has zeros everywhere else. The matrix will now be in reduced row-echelon form.

Example: The system x + y = 1 corresponds to

$$6x - 2z = -8,$$
$$3y - z = -3,$$

the augmented matrix

$$\begin{bmatrix} 1 & 1 & 0 & | & 1 \\ 6 & 0 & -2 & | & -8 \\ 0 & 3 & -1 & | & -3 \end{bmatrix}$$

which reduces to $\begin{bmatrix} 1 & 0 & 0 & | & 1/3 \\ 0 & 1 & 0 & | & 2/3 \\ 0 & 0 & 1 & | & 5 \end{bmatrix}$ which corresponds to

the system $x = \frac{1}{3}$, and the system is solved.

$$y = \frac{2}{3}$$

$$z = 5$$

1.6 ELEMENTARY MATRICES

An N × N matrix which can be derived from the N × N identity matrix by performing a single elementary row operation is called an elementary matrix (E).

9

Theorem:

If E is an M × M elementary matrix and B is an M × N matrix, then the product of EB is equivalent to performing the row operation of E on B.

Theorem:

Every elementary matrix is invertible, and its inverse is also invertible.

Row-equivalent matrices are matrices which can be derived from each other by a finite sequence of row operations.

Theorem:

If A is an N × N matrix, then the following statements are equivalent (either all true or all false):

a) A is invertible.

b) The system of linear equations represented by AX = 0 has only the trivial solution.

c) A is row-equivalent to the N × N identity matrix.

To invert an N × N matrix, A, where N > 2, you must perform the elementary row operations on the N × N identity matrix which would reduce A to I. That derivation of the N × N identity matrix will be A^{-1}.

Theorem:

If A is an invertible N × N matrix, then for the system of equations, AX = B, where B is any N × 1 matrix, there is only one solution; namely $X = A^{-1}B$.

Theorem:

If A is an N × N matrix, then the following statements are equivalent:

a) A is invertible.

b) AX = 0 has only the trivial solution.

c) A is row-equivalent to the N × N identity matrix.

d) AX = B is consistent for every N × N matrix B.

In a homogeneous system, all lines pass through the origin.

CHAPTER 2

DETERMINANTS

2.1 DETERMINANT FUNCTION

A permutation of a set of integers is some arrangement of those integers without any repetitions or omissions.

Example: The permutations of $\{2,3,4\}$ are:

$(2,3,4)$, $(2,4,3)$, $(3,2,4)$, $(3,4,2)$, $(4,2,3)$, $(4,3,2)$.

An inversion in a permutation occurs when a larger integer appears before a smaller one.

Example: $(5,2,3,7)$ There are 2 inversions.

An even permutation has an even number of inversions; an odd permutation has an odd number of inversions.

An elementary product from an $N \times N$ matrix A is a product of N entries from A, with no 2 entries from the same row or column.

Example: $\begin{bmatrix} 1 & 2 \\ 3 & 4 \end{bmatrix}$ The elementary products are 4 and 6.

A signed elementary product from the matrix A is an elementary product of A multiplied by -1 or +1. We use the + sign if the permutation of the set is even and - if odd.

Example: $\begin{bmatrix} 1 & 4 \\ 3 & 2 \end{bmatrix}$ The signed elementary products are 2 and -12.

The determinant of a square matrix A (det(A)) is the sum of all signed elementary products of A.

Example: $\det \begin{bmatrix} 1 & 2 \\ 3 & 4 \end{bmatrix} = (1 \cdot 4) - (2 \cdot 3) = -2$

2.2 DETERMINANTS BY ROW REDUCTION

Theorem:

A square matrix containing a row of zeros has a determinant of zero.

A square matrix is in upper triangular form if it has all zero entries below the main diagonal; it is in lower triangular form if it has all zero entries above the main diagonal; it is in triangular form if it is in either upper or lower triangular form.

Examples: a) $\begin{bmatrix} 1 & 2 & 3 & 4 \\ 0 & 5 & 6 & 7 \\ 0 & 0 & 8 & 9 \\ 0 & 0 & 0 & 10 \end{bmatrix}$ upper triangular form

b) $\begin{bmatrix} 1 & 0 & 0 & 0 \\ 2 & 3 & 0 & 0 \\ 4 & 5 & 6 & 0 \\ 7 & 8 & 9 & 10 \end{bmatrix}$ lower triangular form

Theorem:

If A is an N × N triangular matrix, then the det(a) is the product of the main diagonal entries.

If a square matrix has 2 proportional rows, then its determinant is zero.

Example:
$$\begin{bmatrix} 3 & 4 & 2 \\ 4 & 5 & 1 \\ 6 & 8 & 4 \end{bmatrix} = A$$

$\det(A) = 0$ since the third row is twice the first row.

Theorem:

Given A is any $N \times N$ matrix,

a) if A^* is the result of multiplying one row of A by a constant k, then $\det(A^*) = k\det(A)$.

b) if A^* is the result of switching two rows of A, then $\det(A^*) = -\det(A)$.

c) if A^* is the result of adding a multiple of a row of A to another row of A, then $\det(A^*) = \det(A)$.

Example: The determinant of the reduced non-echelon form of a matrix is equal to the determinant of the matrix.

2.3 DETERMINANT PROPERTIES

If A is an $M \times N$ matrix, then the transpose of A, denoted by (A^t) is defined as the $N \times M$ matrix, where the rows and columns of A are switched.

Example: If $A = \begin{bmatrix} 1 & 2 \\ 2 & 7 \\ 5 & 23 \end{bmatrix}$, then $A^t = \begin{bmatrix} 1 & 2 & 5 \\ 2 & 7 & 23 \end{bmatrix}$.

Properties of the transpose operation

a) $(A^t)^t = A$

b) $(A+B)^t = A^t + B^t$

c) $(kA)^t = kA^t$ (where k is a scalar)

d) $(AB)^t = B^t A^t$

Theorem:

If A is a square matrix, then $\det(A) = \det(A^t)$. (Because of this theorem, all determinant theorems concerning the rows of a matrix also apply to the columns of a matrix.)

If A and B are square matrices of the same size, and k is a scalar, then:

a) $\det(kA) = k^N \det(A)$ (N is the number of rows of A)

b) $\det(AB) = \det(A)\det(B)$

Theorem:

A square matrix A is invertible if and only if $\det(A) \neq 0$.

If A is invertible, then $\det(A^{-1}) = 1/\det(A)$.

2.4 COFACTOR EXPANSION; CRAMER'S RULE

If A is a square matrix, then the minor of entry a_{ij}, denoted (M_{ij}), is defined to be the determinant of the submatrix remaining after the ith row and jth column of A are removed.

Example: $A = \begin{bmatrix} 7 & 1 & 3 \\ 1 & 3 & 5 \\ 17 & 4 & 20 \end{bmatrix}$, $M_{11} = \det \begin{bmatrix} 3 & 5 \\ 4 & 20 \end{bmatrix} = 40$

If A is a square matrix then the cofactor of entry a_{ij}, denoted c_{ij}, is defined to be the scalar $(-1)^{i+j}M_{ij}$.

Example: $A = \begin{bmatrix} 7 & 1 & 3 \\ 1 & 3 & 5 \\ 17 & 4 & 20 \end{bmatrix}$, $c_{11} = (-1)^{1+1}M_{11} = (-1)^2 40 = 40$

$c_{ij} = \pm M_{ij}$, depending on the position of the entry in relation to the matrix

14

$$\begin{bmatrix} + & - & + & - & \cdots \\ - & + & - & + & \cdots \\ + & - & + & - & \cdots \\ - & + & - & + & \cdots \\ \vdots & \vdots & \vdots & \vdots & \end{bmatrix} \cdot$$

Examples: $C_{11} = +M_{11}$, $C_{12} = -M_{12}$, $C_{43} = -M_{43}$, etc.

If A is a square matrix, det(A) can be found by cofactor expansion along the ith row or jth column of A. This is done by multiplying the entries in the ith row of the jth column of A by their cofactors and summing the resulting products. Thus,

$$\det(A) = a_{i1}C_{i1} + a_{i2}C_{i2} + \ldots$$

or

$$\det(A) = a_{1j}C_{2j} + a_{2j}C_{2j} + \ldots$$

Example: expansion along first row;

$$\det \begin{bmatrix} 2 & 4 & 3 \\ 7 & 2 & 12 \\ 1 & 3 & 9 \end{bmatrix} = (2)(-18) + 4(-51) + (3)(19) = -183$$

If A is a square matrix and c_{ij} is the cofactor of a_{ij}, then the matrix of cofactors from A is:

$$\begin{bmatrix} c_{11} & c_{12} & \cdots \\ c_{21} & c_{22} & \cdots \\ \vdots & \vdots & \end{bmatrix}$$

The transpose of this matrix is called the adjoint of A (adj(A)).

Theorem:

If A is an invertible matrix, then:

$$A^{-1} = \frac{1}{\det(A)} \ adj(A)$$

15

CRAMER'S RULE

If $AX = B$ is a system of N linear equations having unknowns $X_1, X_2, \ldots, X_N$, then the unique solution of the system is:

$$X_1 = \frac{\det(A_1)}{\det(A)}, \quad X_2 = \frac{\det(A_2)}{\det(A)} \quad \cdots, \quad X_N = \frac{\det(A_N)}{\det(A)}$$

where A_N is the matrix obtained by replacing the jth column of A with the column of constants of the system,

$$B = \begin{bmatrix} b_1 \\ b_2 \\ \vdots \\ b_N \end{bmatrix}.$$

2.5 WHAT THE DETERMINANT MEASURES

The absolute value of the determinant of a 2×2 matrix measure how much area is distorted by the linear transformation represented by the matrix.

Example: If T is represented by $\begin{bmatrix} 1 & 2 \\ 0 & 2 \end{bmatrix}$ then

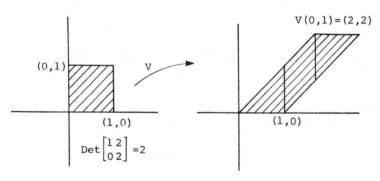

$V(0,1) = (2,2)$

$(0,1)$

V

$(1,0)$

$(1,0)$

$\text{Det} \begin{bmatrix} 1 & 2 \\ 0 & 2 \end{bmatrix} = 2$

16

Under the transformation T, the area of the unit square has gone from 1 to 2.1.

This gives a visual demonstration of why the determinant of a matrix with two rows which are multiples of each other is zero. In this case, the unit box is mapped to a line which has zero area.

Example: Let $A = [2 \ \ 2]$

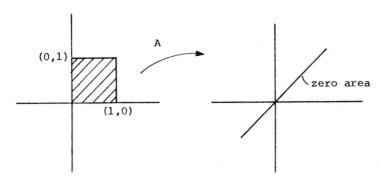

The determinant of a 3 × 3 matrix measures how much volume is distorted.

CHAPTER 3

VECTOR SPACES

3.1 EUCLIDEAN N-SPACE

An ordered N-tuple is a sequence of N real numbers, where N is a positive integer. An ordered 2-tuple is called an ordered pair and an ordered 3-tuple is called an ordered triple.

Example: $(4, 7, 12, 9, 3)$ is an ordered 5-tuple.

The N-space ($\mathbb{R}^N$) is the set of all ordered N-tuples. $\mathbb{R}^1$ is the set of all real numbers and can be written as $\mathbb{R}$.

3.2 VECTOR SPACES

Let V be a set of objects on which two operations are defined, addition and multiplication by scalars (real numbers. Let it also be given that a, b and c are members of V, and x and y are scalars. If V conforms to the following rules, then V is called a vector space, and a, b and c are called vectors:

a) $a + b \in V$.

b) $a + b = b + a$

c) a + (b+c) = (a+b) + c

d) The zero vector 0 is an element of V such that $0 + a = a$.

e) The negative of a, -a, is an element of V such that a+(-a) = 0.

f) Xa ∈ V

g) x(a+b) = xa + xb

h) (x+y)a = xa + ya

i) x(ya) = (xy)a

j) 1a = a

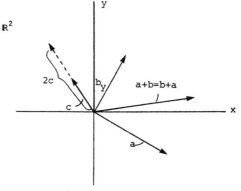

Fig. 1 R^2 is a vector space.

To efficiently test if an object v is a vector you must check to find if all of the following hold for v (for easy identification, all vectors are identified by arrows above the letters):

a) $\vec{0}\vec{v} = \vec{0}$

b) $k\vec{0} = \vec{0}$

c) $(-1)\vec{v} = -\vec{v}$

d) If $k\vec{v} = \vec{0}$, then $k = 0$ or $\vec{v} = \vec{0}$

A vector space can be in the form of N-space, with its vectors in the form of N-tuples. For this representation, the following apply:

a) Two vectors $\vec{a} = (a_1, a_2, \ldots, a_N)$ and $\vec{b} = (b_1, b_2, \ldots, b_N)$ in R^N are equal if $a_1 = b_1$, $a_2 = b_2, \ldots, a_N = b_N$.

b) The sum a + b is defined to be

$$\vec{a} + \vec{b} = (a_1 + b_1, a_2 + b_2, \ldots, a_N + b_N).$$

19

c) If L is a scalar, then the scalar multiple is defined to be
$$L\vec{a} = (La_1, La_2, \ldots, La_N).$$

d) The zero vector is defined to be $\vec{0} = (0, 0, \ldots, 0)$.

e) The negative of $\vec{a}$ is defined to be

$$-\vec{a} = (-a_1, -a_2, \ldots, -a_N).$$

f) $\vec{a} - \vec{b} = \vec{a} + (-\vec{b})$.

A vector space in $\mathbb{R}^1$, $\mathbb{R}^2$ or $\mathbb{R}^3$ can be represented in a geometric form, with a line, a plane, or two planes representing the vector space and either dots or lines representing the vectors.

Examples: a) $\vec{v} = (4)$ in $\mathbb{R}^1$

b) $\vec{u} = (6,3)$ in $\mathbb{R}^2$

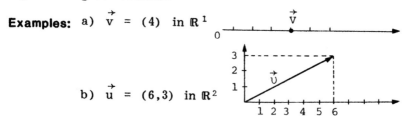

3.3 SUBSPACES

Let V be a vector space, and let W be a subset of V. W is itself a vector space, and thus a subspace of v if W satisfies the following conditions:

a) If v and w are elements of W, then their sum $v + w$ is also an element of W.

b) If v is an element of W and c is a number, then cv is an element of W.

c) The element 0 of v is also an element of W.

Every vector space has at least two subspaces; the vector space itself, and the zero subspace (the space consisting of the zero vector only).

The vector consisting of a solution of a system of linear equations is called the solution vector of the system.

The set of all solution vectors is called the solution space of the system.

Example: $x_1 = 3$ solution vector $= (3,2)$

$\qquad x_1 + x_2 = 5$

A vector $\vec{w}$ is called a linear combination of the vectors $\vec{v}_1, \vec{v}_2, \ldots, \vec{v}_n$ if $\vec{w} = k_1\vec{v}_1 + k_2\vec{v}_2 + \ldots + k_n\vec{v}_n$,

where $k_1, k_2, \ldots, k_n$ are scalars.

Example: If $\vec{w} = (10,24,54)$ and $\vec{v}_1 = (1,2,3)$ and $\vec{v}_2 = (2,5,12)$, then $\vec{w}$ is a linear combination of $\vec{v}_1$ and $\vec{v}_2$ since

$$\vec{w} = 2\vec{v}_1 + 4\vec{v}_2 = 2<1,2,3> + 4<2,5,12> = <2,4,6>$$

$$+ <8,20,48> = <10,24,54> \, .$$

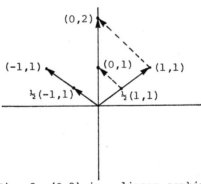

Fig. 2 (0,2) is a linear combination of (1,1) and (-1,1), and (0,1) is also $(0,1)=\frac{1}{2}(1,1)+\frac{1}{2}(-1,1)$.

If every vector in a vector space V can be expressed as a linear combination of a subspace of V, then the vectors in that subspace are said to span V.

Theorem:

If $\vec{x}_1, \vec{x}_2, \ldots, \vec{x}_n$ are vectors in the vector space X, then:

21

a) the set Y of all linear combinations of $\vec{x}_1, \vec{x}_2, \ldots, \vec{x}_n$ is a subspace of X.

b) Y is the smallest subset of X which contains $\vec{x}_1, \vec{x}_2, \ldots, \vec{x}_n$.

The vector space spanned by the set of vectors in a vector space V is called the linear space of V, denoted by (lin(V)).

3.4 LINEAR INDEPENDENCE

Let V be a vector space, and let $v_1 \ldots, v_n$ be elements of V. Vectors $v_1, \ldots, v_n$ are linearly dependent if there exists numbers $a_1, \ldots, a_n$ not all equal to zero such that,

$$a_1 v_1 + \ldots + a_n v_n = 0.$$

If such numbers do not exist, then $v_1, \ldots, v_n$ are linearly independent.

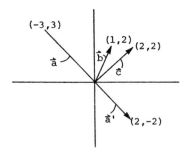

Fig. 3
$\vec{a}$ and $\vec{a}'$ are linearly dependent since $-1\vec{a}=\vec{a}'$.

$\vec{a}, \vec{b}, \vec{c}$ or $\vec{a}', \vec{b}, \vec{c}$ are a linearly dependent set of vectors since $\vec{b}=-\frac{1}{4}\vec{a}+\frac{3}{4}\vec{c}$.

If $z = \{\vec{Z}_1, \vec{Z}_2, \ldots, \vec{Z}_R\}$ is a set of vectors in $\mathbb{R}^N$, and $R > n$, then z is linearly dependent.

22

3.5 BASIS AND DIMENSION

If V is any vector space and $x = \{v_1, v_2, v_3, \ldots, v_R\}$ is a finite set of vectors in V, then s is called a basis for V. Also:

a) x is linearly independent

b) x spans V

Example: $V = \{(1,0,0),(0,1,0),(0,0,1)\}$ is the basis for $\mathbb{R}^3$

The set of vectors $\{(1,0,\ldots,0),(0,1,0,\ldots,0),\ldots,(0,0,\ldots,1)\}$ in $\mathbb{R}^n$ is called the standard basis for $\mathbb{R}^n$.

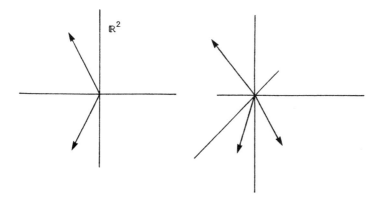

Fig. 4 Any two non-colinear vectors in $\mathbb{R}^2$ span $\mathbb{R}^3$.

Fig. 5 Any three non-coplanar vectors in $\mathbb{R}^3$ span $\mathbb{R}^3$.

If a non-zero vector space contains a basis consisting of a finite set of vectors, then it is called finite dimensional. Otherwise, it is infinite dimensional. The zero vector space is defined to be finite dimensional.

Theorem:

Any 2 bases for a finite dimensional vector space must have the same number of vectors.

The number of vectors in a basis of a finite dimensional vector space is called the dimension of that vector space. The zero vector space is said to have dimension zero.

Theorem:

If $s = \{v_1, v_2, \ldots, v_r\}$ is a linearly independent set of vectors in an N-dimensional space x, and R < n, then s can be enlarged to form a basis for V.

3.6 ROW AND COLUMN SPACE OF A MATRIX

Given the M × N matrix

$$A = \begin{bmatrix} a_{11} & a_{12} & \cdots & a_{1N} \\ a_{21} & a_{22} & \cdots & a_{2N} \\ \vdots & \vdots & & \vdots \\ a_{M1} & a_{M2} & \cdots & a_{MN} \end{bmatrix}$$

a) The vectors $(a_{11}, a_{12}, \ldots, a_{1N})$, $(a_{21}, a_{22}, \ldots, a_{2N})$, ..., $(a_{M1}, a_{M2}, \ldots, a_{MN})$ are called the row vectors of A.

b) The vectors $(a_{11}, a_{21}, \ldots, a_{M1})$, $(a_{12}, a_{22}, \ldots, a_{M2})$, ..., $(a_{1N}, a_{2N}, \ldots, a_{MN})$ are called the column vectors of A.

c) The row space of A is the subspace of $\mathbb{R}^N$ spanned by the row vectors.

d) The column space of A is the subspace of $\mathbb{R}^M$ spanned by the column vectors.

Theorem:

Elementary row operations do not change the row space of a matrix.

Theorem:

The non-zero row vectors from the row-echelon form of a matrix form a basis for the row space of that matrix.

Theorem:

The row space and column space of a matrix have the same dimension.

The rank of a matrix is defined to be the dimension of the row space and column space of that matrix.

Example: The rank of $\begin{bmatrix} 1 & 0 & 1 & 1 \\ 3 & 2 & 5 & 1 \\ 0 & 4 & 4 & -4 \end{bmatrix}$ is 2.

Theorem:

If A is an $N \times N$ matrix, then the following statements are equivalent:

a) A is invertible.

b) $A\vec{X} = \vec{0}$ has only the trivial solution.

c) A is row-equivalent to the $N \times N$ identity matrix.

d) $A\vec{X} = b$ is consistent for every $N \times 1$ matrix b.

e) $\det(A) \neq 0$.

f) A has rank N.

g) The row and column vectors of A are linearly independent.

3.7 INNER PRODUCT SPACES

An inner product on a vector space V produces a real number $<\vec{v}_1, \vec{v}_2>$ from each pair of vectors $\vec{v}_1, \vec{v}_2 \in$ V, which satisfies the following axioms for all vectors $\vec{v}_1, \vec{v}_2, \vec{v}_3 \in$ V and for all scalars L.

a) $<\vec{v}_1, \vec{v}_2> = <\vec{v}_2, \vec{v}_1>$

b) $< \vec{v}_1 + \vec{v}_2, \vec{v}_3 > = < \vec{v}_1, \vec{v}_3 > + < \vec{v}_2, \vec{v}_3 >$

c) $< L\vec{v}_1, \vec{v}_2 > = L < \vec{v}_1, \vec{v}_2 >$

d) $< \vec{v}_1, \vec{v}_1 > \geq 0$ and $< \vec{v}_1, \vec{v}_1 > = 0$, if and only if $\vec{v} = \vec{0}$.

If $X = (x_1, x_2, \ldots, x_N)$ and $Y = (y_1, y_2, \ldots, y_N)$ are vectors in $\mathbb{R}^N$, then the Euclidean inner product is defined as:

$$< \vec{X}, \vec{Y} > = X_1 Y_1 + X_2 Y_2 + \ldots + X_N Y_N$$

Example: If $X = (2, 4, 6)$ and $Y = (7, 1, 1)$ then

$$< X, Y > = 14 + 4 + 6 = 24.$$

A vector space with an inner product is called an inner product space.

3.7.1 CAUCHY-SCHWARZ INEQUALITY

If a and b are vectors in an inner product space, then:

$$< \vec{a}, \vec{b} >^2 \leq < \vec{a}, \vec{a} > < \vec{b}, \vec{b} >$$

3.8 LENGTH AND ANGLE IN INNER PRODUCT SPACES

If V is an inner product space, then the norm (or length) of a vector $\vec{a} \in V$ is defined as:

$$\| \vec{a} \| = < \vec{a}, \vec{a} >^{\frac{1}{2}}$$

Example: If $\vec{a} = (3, 2, 6)$, then $\| \vec{a} \| = 7$.

If V is an inner product space, then the distance between two vectors $a, b \in V$ is defined as:

$$d(\vec{a}, \vec{b}) = \| \vec{a} - \vec{b} \|$$

Example: If $\vec{a} = (1,9,2)$ and $b = (7,7,1)$, then $d(\vec{a},\vec{b}) = \sqrt{41}$.

Theorem:

If V is an inner product space, $\vec{a}$, $\vec{b}$ and $\vec{c}$ are vectors in V, and L is a scalar, then:

a) $\| \vec{a} \| \geq 0$ $\qquad\qquad$ $d(\vec{a},\vec{b}) \geq 0$

b) $\| \vec{a} \| = 0$, if and only $\qquad$ $d(\vec{a},\vec{b})=0$, if and only if $\vec{a}=\vec{b}$
if $\vec{a} = \vec{0}$

c) $\| L\vec{a} \| = |L| \, \| \vec{a} \|$ $\qquad\qquad$ $d(\vec{a},\vec{b}) = d(\vec{b},\vec{a})$

d) $\| \vec{a}+\vec{b} \| \leq \| \vec{a} \| + \| \vec{b} \|$ $\qquad$ $d(\vec{a},\vec{b}) \leq d(\vec{a},\vec{c}) + d(\vec{c},\vec{b})$

The angle between two vectors $\vec{a}$ and $\vec{b}$ in an inner product space V is defined as:

$$\theta = \text{arc cos} \left(\frac{<\vec{a},\vec{b}>}{\| \vec{a} \| \, \| \vec{b} \|} \right) \quad \text{where} \quad 0 \leq \theta \leq \pi$$

Two vectors $\vec{a}$ and $\vec{b}$ in an inner product space are orthogonal if $<\vec{a},\vec{b}> = 0$. If $\vec{a}$ is orthogonal to each vector in a set of vectors X, then $\vec{a}$ is orthogonal to X.

Example: The vectors $(1,2,-3)$ and $(-3,9,5)$ are orthogonal.

$$1(-3) + 2(9) + (-3)5 = -3 + 18 - 15 = 0$$

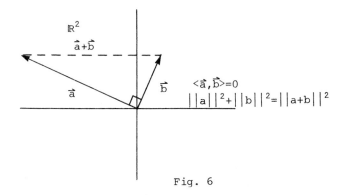

Fig. 6

27

Theorem:

If $\vec{a}$ and $\vec{b}$ are orthogonal vectors in an inner product space, then:

$$\| \vec{a+b} \|^2 = \| \vec{a} \|^2 + \| \vec{b} \|^2$$

3.9 ORTHONORMAL BASES

If, in a set of vectors, in an inner product space, all pairs of distinct vectors are orthogonal, then the set is called an orthogonal set.

An orthonormal set is an orthogonal set in which each vector has a norm of one.

The process of multiplying a non-zero vector by the reciprocal of its norm to make it orthonormal is called normalizing the vector.

Theorem:

If $V = \{\vec{v}_1, \vec{v}_2, \ldots, \vec{v}_N\}$ is an orthonormal basis for an inner product space X, and a $\in$ X, then:

$$\vec{a} = <\vec{a}, \vec{v}_1> \vec{v}_1 + <\vec{a}, \vec{v}_2> \vec{v}_2 + \ldots + <\vec{a}, \vec{v}_N> \vec{v}_N$$

Theorem:

If $V = \{\vec{v}_1, \vec{v}_2, \ldots, \vec{v}_N\}$ is a non-zero, orthogonal set, in an inner product space, then V is linearly independent.

If $V = \{\vec{v}_1, \vec{v}_2, \ldots \vec{v}_N\}$ is an orthonormal set of vectors in an inner product space X, and if Y is the space spanned by V, then every vector $\vec{a} \in$ X can be expressed in the form $\vec{a} = \vec{y}_1 + \vec{y}_2$, where $\vec{y}_1 \in$ Y is called the orthogonal projection of $\vec{a}$ on X. $\vec{y}_2$ is orthogonal to Y and

28

is called the component of $\vec{a}$ orthogonal to Y. $\vec{y}_1$ and $\vec{y}_2$ are calculated as follows:

a) $\vec{y}_1 = <\vec{a},\vec{v}_1>\vec{v}_1 + <\vec{a},\vec{v}_2>\vec{v}_2 + \ldots + <\vec{a},\vec{v}_N>\vec{v}_N$

b) $\vec{y}_2 = \vec{a} - <\vec{a},\vec{v}_1>\vec{v}_1 - <\vec{a},\vec{v}_2>\vec{v}_2 - \ldots - <\vec{a},\vec{v}_N>\vec{v}_N$

Theorem;

Every non-zero, finite dimensional inner product space has a basis consisting of orthonormal vectors, called an orthonormal basis.

3.9.1 GRAM-SCHMIDT PROCESS

Converts any basis $\{\vec{a}_1,\vec{a}_2,\ldots,\vec{a}_N\}$ into an orthonormal basis $\{\vec{v}_1,\vec{v}_2,\ldots,\vec{v}_N\}$.

a) Let $\vec{v}_1 = \vec{a}_1/\|\vec{a}_1\|$. $\vec{v}_1$ will have a norm of one.

b) Construct $\vec{v}_2 = \dfrac{\vec{a}_2 - <\vec{a}_2,\vec{v}_1>\vec{v}_1}{\|\vec{a}_2 - <\vec{a}_2,\vec{v}_1>\vec{v}_1\|}$

c) Construct $\vec{v}_3 = \dfrac{\vec{a}_3 - <\vec{a}_3,\vec{v}_1>\vec{v}_1 - <\vec{a}_3,\vec{v}_2>\vec{v}_2}{\|\vec{a}_3 - <\vec{a}_3,\vec{v}_1>\vec{v}_1 - <\vec{a}_3,\vec{v}_2>\vec{v}_2\|}$

Continue until an orthonormal set of vectors $\{\vec{v}_1,\vec{v}_2,\ldots\vec{v}_N\}$ is obtained. This will be the orthonormal basis.

3.10 COORDINATES AND CHANGE OF BASIS

If $V = \{\vec{v}_1,\vec{v}_2,\ldots,\vec{v}_N\}$ is a basis for the vector space X, then every vector a $\in$ X can be expressed as $\vec{a} = c_1\vec{v}_1 + c_2\vec{v}_2 + \ldots + c_N\vec{v}_N$, where the scalars $c_1,c_2,\ldots,c_N$ are called the coordinates of X relative to V. The coordinate matrix is the N × 1 matrix

$$\begin{bmatrix} c_1 \\ c_2 \\ \vdots \\ c_N \end{bmatrix} = (\vec{a})_v.$$

Theorem:

If V is an orthonormal basis for an inner product space and if $(\vec{X})_S = (x_1, x_2, \ldots, x_N)$ and $(\vec{Y})_S = (y_1, y_2, \ldots, y_N)$, then:

a) $\| \vec{x} \| = (x_1^2 + x_2^2 + \ldots + x_N^2)^{\frac{1}{2}}$

b) $d(\vec{X}, \vec{Y}) = \left((x_1 - y_1)^2 + (x_2 - y_2)^2 + \ldots + (x_N - y_N)^2 \right)^{\frac{1}{2}}$

c) $< \vec{X}, \vec{Y} > = x_1 y_1 + x_2 y_2 + \ldots + x_N y_N$

If the basis for a vector space V is being changed from $W = \{\vec{w}_1, \vec{w}_2, \ldots, \vec{w}_N\}$ to $S = \{\vec{s}_1, \vec{s}_2, \ldots, \vec{s}_N\}$, then the transition matrix is defined as:

$$P = \left[(\vec{w}_1)_S \vdots (\vec{w}_2)_S \vdots \ldots \vdots (\vec{w}_n)_S \right]$$

where $(\vec{w}_j)_S = (C_{1j}, C_{2j}, \ldots, C_{nj})$

$j = 1, 2, \ldots, n$ s.t. $wj = C_{1j} S_1 + C_{2j} S_2 + \ldots + C_{nj} S_n$

P is invertible, and P^{-1} is the transition matrix from S to W.

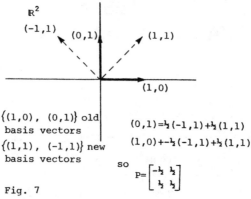

$\mathbb{R}^2$

$(-1,1)$ $(0,1)$ $(1,1)$

$(1,0)$

$\{(1,0), (0,1)\}$ old basis vectors

$\{(1,1), (-1,1)\}$ new basis vectors

$(0,1) = \frac{1}{2}(-1,1) + \frac{1}{2}(1,1)$

$(1,0) + -\frac{1}{2}(-1,1) + \frac{1}{2}(1,1)$

so $P = \begin{bmatrix} -\frac{1}{2} & \frac{1}{2} \\ \frac{1}{2} & \frac{1}{2} \end{bmatrix}$

Fig. 7

30

Theorem:

If P is the transition matrix from one orthonormal basis to another, then $P^{-1} = P^t$.

The square matrix A with the property $A^{-1} + A^t$ is called an orthogonal matrix.

Theorem:

If A is an $N \times N$ matrix, then the following are equivalent:

a) A is orthogonal.

b) The row and column vectors of A form an orthonormal set in $\mathbb{R}^N$.

CHAPTER 4

LINEAR TRANSFORMATIONS

4.1 LINEAR TRANSFORMATIONS

If V and X are vector spaces and F is a function that relates a vector in V with a unique vector in X, then F is said to map X into V; $F:X \rightarrow V$.

If F is a function that associates a vector $\vec{a}$ with a vector $\vec{b}$, then $\vec{a}$ is the image of $\vec{b}$ under F.

If F is a function mapping the vector space X into the vector space Y, then F is called a linear transformation if:

a) $F(\vec{a}+\vec{b}) = F(\vec{a}) + F(\vec{b})$, for all $\vec{a},\vec{b} \in X$

b) $F(L\vec{a}) = LF(\vec{a})$ for all $\vec{a} \in X$, and scalars L.

If A is an M × N matrix and B is an N × 1 matrix, then the matrix transformation function T(B) is defined as:

$$T(B) = AB$$

Example: If $A = \begin{bmatrix} 2 & 3 \\ 4 & 1 \end{bmatrix}$ and $B = \begin{bmatrix} 1 \\ 2 \end{bmatrix}$, then $T(B) = AB$

$$= \begin{bmatrix} 5 \\ 6 \end{bmatrix}.$$

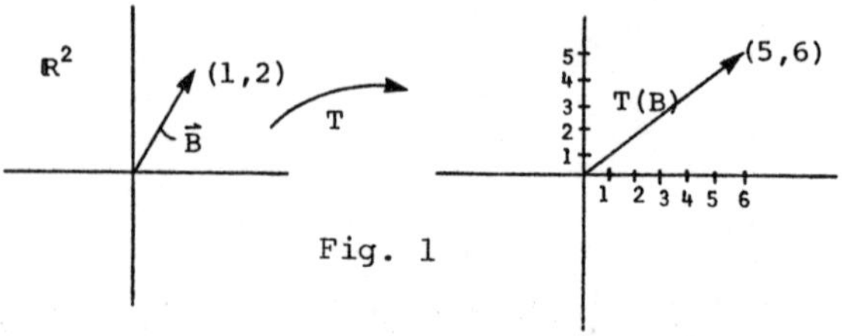

Fig. 1

If V is a vector space, then the function $T(\vec{a}) = \vec{0}$ for all $\vec{a} \in V$ is called the zero transformation.

If V is a vector space, then the function $T(\vec{a}) = \vec{a}$ for every $\vec{a} \in V$ is called the identity transformation.

If V is a vector space and L is a scalar, then the function $T(\vec{a}) = L\vec{a}$ for every $\vec{a} \in V$ is called a dilation of V if $L > 1$, or a contraction of V if $0 < L < 1$.

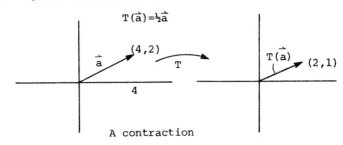

A contraction

Fig.2

If V is an inner product space, and if $\{\vec{X}_1, \vec{X}_2, \ldots, \vec{X}_N\}$ is an orthonormal basis of X, a finite dimensional subspace of V, then the function

$$T(\vec{a}) = <\vec{a_1 x_1}> \vec{x}_1 + <\vec{a_1 x_2}> \vec{x}_2 + \ldots + <\vec{a_1 x}_n> \vec{x}_N$$

for every $\vec{a} \in V$ is called the orthogonal projection of V into X.

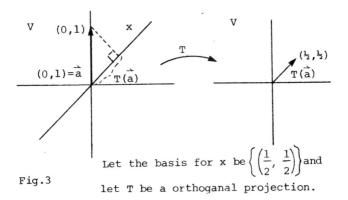

Let the basis for x be $\left\{\left(\frac{1}{2}, \frac{1}{2}\right)\right\}$ and let T be a orthoganal projection.

Fig.3

4.2 KERNEL AND RANGE

Theorem:

If $T:A \to B$ is a linear transformation with $\vec{a} \in A$ and $\vec{b} \in B$, then:

a) $T(\vec{0}) = \vec{0}$

b) $T(-\vec{a}) = -T(\vec{a})$

c) $T(\vec{a}-\vec{b}) = T(\vec{a}) - T(\vec{b})$

The kernel (or null space) of a linear transformation $T(Ker(t))$ is that set of vectors which T maps into $\vec{0}$.

Example: If $T:A \to B$ is a zero transformation, then the vector space A is the kernel of T.

$$\text{Ker } T = \{\, a \in A \mid T(a) = \vec{0}\,\} = T^{-1}(\vec{0})$$

The range of linear transformation $T:A \to B$, $(R(T))$, is the set of vectors in B that are images under T of at least one vector in A.

$$\text{IMT} = \text{RANGE } T = \{b \in B \quad a \in A \text{ s.t. } T(a)=b\}$$

Example: If $T:A \to B$ is a zero transformation, then $R(T) = \vec{0}$.

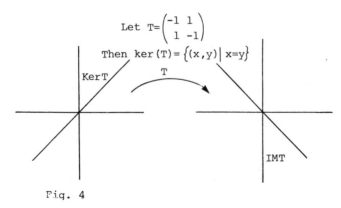

Let $T=\begin{pmatrix} -1 & 1 \\ 1 & -1 \end{pmatrix}$

Then $\ker(T) = \{(x,y) \mid x=y\}$

Fig. 4

34

If $T: \mathbb{R}^N \to \mathbb{R}^M$ represents multiplication by an $M \times N$ matrix A, then Ker(t) is the solution space of A; R(T) is the column space of A.

If T is a linear transformation, then dim(R(T)) is called the rank of T, and dim(Ker(T)) is called the nullity of T.

Theorem:

If A is an n-dimensional vector space and $T: A \to B$ is a linear transformation, then

$$(\text{rank of } T) + (\text{nullity of } T) = N.$$

Theorem:

If A is an $M \times N$ matrix, then the dimensions of the solution space of $A\vec{X} = \vec{0}$ equal N-(rank of A).

4.3 LINEAR TRANSFORMATIONS FROM $\mathbb{R}^N$ TO $\mathbb{R}^M$

For every linear transformation $T: \mathbb{R}^N \to \mathbb{R}^M$, with $\{\vec{v}_1, \vec{v}_2, \ldots, \vec{v}_N\}$ being the standard basis for $\mathbb{R}^N$, there is an $M \times N$ matrix A, called the standard matrix for T, for which T is a multiple of A. A has $\{T(\vec{v}_1), T(\vec{v}_2), \ldots, T(\vec{v}_N)\}$ as its column vectors:

$$A = \left[T(\vec{v}_1) \vdots T(\vec{v}_2) \vdots \ldots \vdots T(\vec{v}_N) \right]$$

Example: If $B = \begin{bmatrix} x \\ y \\ z \end{bmatrix}$, then for $T(A) = \begin{bmatrix} x-z \\ x+y \\ y+z \\ y \end{bmatrix}$

the standard matrix is

$$A = \begin{bmatrix} 1 & 0 & -1 \\ 1 & 1 & 0 \\ 0 & 1 & 1 \\ 0 & 1 & 0 \end{bmatrix}.$$

The standard matrix for a matrix transformation is the matrix itself.

4.4 MATRICES OF LINEAR TRANSFORMATIONS

If A is an n-dimensional vector space with basis $S = \{\vec{s}_1, \vec{s}_2, \ldots, \vec{s}_n\}$, and B is an m-dimensional vector space with basis $Z = \{\vec{z}_1, \vec{z}_2, \ldots, \vec{z}_m\}$, then for the transformation $T:A \to B$, the matrix of T with respect to the bases S and Z is defined as:

$$\left[T(\vec{s}_1)_z \quad T(\vec{s}_2)_z \quad \ldots \quad T(\vec{s}_n)_z \right]$$

$$TC(s_j)_z = \begin{bmatrix} c_1 \\ \vdots \\ c_m \end{bmatrix} \text{ s.t.}$$

$$T(\vec{s}_j) = c_1 z_1 + c_2 z_2 + \ldots + c_m z_m$$

If V is a vector space with a finite basis S, then for $T:V \to V_1$ the matrix of T with respect to the basis S will be just the standard matrix for T.

4.5 SIMILARITY

Let V be a finite dimensional vector space and $T:V \rightarrow V$ its linear operator. If A is the matrix of T with respect to a basis X, and B is the matrix of T with respect to a matrix Y, and if P is the transition matrix from X to Y, then $B = PAP^{-1}$.

If A and B are square matrices, then A and B are similar if an invertible matrix P exists such that $B = PAP^{-1}$.

CHAPTER 5

EIGENVALUES, EIGENVECTORS

5.1 EIGENVALUES, EIGENVECTORS

If A is an N × N matrix, then the non-zero vector $\vec{X}$ $\in \mathbb{R}^N$ is called an eigenvector of A if $A\vec{x} = \lambda\vec{x}$, where λ is a scalar called the eigenvalue of A.

If A is a square matrix, then the characteristic equation of A is defined to be $\det(\lambda I - A) = 0$. When expanded, the $\det(\lambda I - A)$ is called the characteristic polynomial of A.

5.2 DIAGONALIZATION

If A is a square matrix and there exists a matrix B such that $B^{-1}AB$ is diagonal, then A is diagonalizable and B diagonalizes A.

Theorem:

If A is an N × N matrix and A is diagonalizable, then A has N linearly independent eigenvectors.

The following is the procedure for diagonalizing an N × N matrix A:

a) Find the set of N linearly independent eigenvectors of A, $\{\vec{v}_1, \vec{v}_2, \ldots, \vec{v}_n\}$

b) Form the matrix P having $\vec{v}_1, \vec{v}_2, \ldots, \vec{v}_N$ as its column vectors.

c) The matrix $P^{-1}AP$ will then be diagonal, with $\lambda_1, \lambda_2, \ldots, \lambda_N$ as its diagonal entries where λ_i is the eigenvalue corresponding $\vec{V}_i$, i = 1, 2, ..., n.

Theorem:

If $\vec{v}_1, \vec{v}_2, \ldots, \vec{v}_N$ are eigenvectors corresponding to distinct eigenvalues $\lambda_1, \lambda_2, \ldots, \lambda_N$, then $\{\vec{v}_1, \vec{v}_2, \ldots, \vec{v}_N\}$ is a linearly independent set.

Theorem:

If an N × N matrix has N distinct eigenvalues, then it is diagonalizable.

5.3 SYMMETRIC MATRICES

A square matrix A is said to be orthogonally diagonalizable if there is an orthogonal matrix P such that $P^{-1}AP$ is diagonal. The matrix P is said to orthogonally diagonalize A.

The matrix A with the property $A = A^t$ is said to be symmetric.

Example: $\begin{bmatrix} 1 & 2 \\ 2 & 1 \end{bmatrix}$ is a symmetric matrix.

The following is the procedure for orthogonally diagonalizing a symmetric matrix A:

a) Find a basis for each eigenspace of A.

b) Find an orthonormal basis for each eigenspace by applying the Gram-Schmidt process to each basis.

c) Form the matrix P using the orthonormal bases as column vectors; P orthogonally diagonalizes A.

Theorem:

a) The characteristic equation of a symmetric matrix A has only real roots.

b) If an eigenvalue λ of a symmetric matrix is repeated L times as a root of the characteristic equation, then the eigenspace corresponding to λ is L-dimensional.